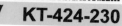

Learning Points

- Children love big machines of any kind and it's fascinating for them to recognise and learn more about these machines in their own books.

- This book is designed to help you to explain what machines are for – and introduce your child to the way they work.

- Take time to look at the details in the pictures. Can your child remember what each machine is called?

- Go on a big machine hunt together – see how many you can find.

Ladybird books are widely available, but in case of difficulty may be ordered by post or telephone from:

Ladybird Books – Cash Sales Department
Littlegate Road Paignton Devon TQ3 3BE
Telephone 01803 554761

A catalogue record for this book is available
from the British Library

Published by Ladybird Books Ltd Loughborough Leicestershire UK
Ladybird Books Inc Auburn Maine 04210 USA

let's look at

Big
Machines

by Karen Bryant-Mole
illustrated by Stuart Trotter

Excavators

Excavators are sometimes called diggers. Their job is to scoop up earth. This excavator is digging a long trench.

Can you see the levers the driver is holding? He is using these to make the excavator work.

Concrete Mixers

The drum on the back of this
concrete mixer turns round and
round. It mixes together sand,
cement, stones and water to
make concrete.

The concrete is pouring out of the mixer. When it sets it will be as hard as rock.

Road Rollers

A new road is being laid. The rollers on a road roller are smooth and very heavy. They press down on the road to make sure that it is flat.

Road rollers can be very noisy.
Can you see what the driver is
wearing over his ears?

Tipper Trucks

This tipper truck is delivering sand to a building site. The back of the truck is tipping up and all the sand is sliding out.

How are the builders going
to move the sand?
What do you think they
are building?

Cranes

Cranes are used to move heavy objects. This crane is lifting a big metal bar. The bar is part of a new building.

Look out for a crane
next time you go past
a building site.

Transporters

This transporter carries new cars. It takes them from the factory where they are made to the showrooms and garages where they will be sold.

How many cars can you count on the transporter?

Petrol Tankers

This tanker carries petrol to the petrol station. The driver uses a hose to fill big underground tanks with petrol.

Have you ever been to a
petrol station?

Tractors

Tractors have great big wheels that help them drive over fields. This tractor is pulling a special tool called a plough.

Look at the birds trying to catch the earthworms!

Combine Harvesters

This farmer is cutting wheat with a combine harvester. The wheat is shaken off the stalks and collected inside the machine.

Wheat makes flour for bread
and pastry.
Have you seen flour at home?

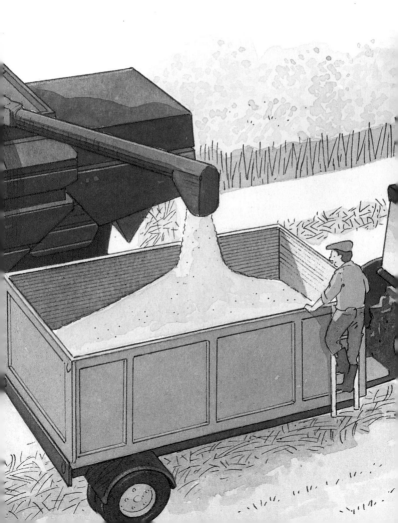

Dustcarts

Dustcarts take away the rubbish that people leave in bins and bags by their gates. The refuse collectors throw the rubbish into the dustcart.

Inside the dustcart a large metal presser squashes the rubbish.

Snow Ploughs

Snow ploughs help to clear the roads when there is heavy snow. The scoop at the front pushes the snow to the side of the road.

How many cars are waiting for
the snow plough to clear
their way?

Hovercraft

A hovercraft skims over water on a cushion of air. This hovercraft is crossing the sea.

Its propellors are spinning. How many propellors can you count?

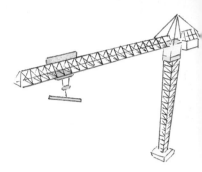